INTRODUCING
Marxism

Rupert Woodfin • Oscar Zarate

Edited by Richard Appignanesi

Icon Books UK ◆ Totem Books USA

Published in the UK in 2004
by Icon Books Ltd.,
The Old Dairy, Brook Road,
Thriplow, Royston SG8 7RG
email: info@iconbooks.co.uk
www.iconbooks.co.uk

Published in the USA in 2004
by Totem Books
Inquiries to: Icon Books Ltd.,
The Old Dairy, Brook Road,
Thriplow, Royston
SG8 7RG, UK

Sold in the UK, Europe, South Africa
and Asia by Faber and Faber Ltd.,
3 Queen Square, London WC1N 3AU
or their agents

Distributed to the trade in the USA by
National Book Network Inc.,
4720 Boston Way, Lanham,
Maryland 20706

Distributed in the UK, Europe, South
Africa and Asia by TBS Ltd., Frating
Distribution Centre, Colchester Road,
Frating Green, Colchester CO7 7DW

Distributed in Canada by
Penguin Books Canada,
10 Alcorn Avenue, Suite 300,
Toronto, Ontario M4V 3B2

Published in Australia in 2004 by
Allen and Unwin Pty. Ltd., PO Box
8500, 83 Alexander Street, Crows
Nest, NSW 2065

ISBN 1 84046 462 3

Originating editor: Richard Appignanesi

Printed and bound in Singapore
by Tien Wah Press Ltd.

The Origins

In February 1848, Karl Marx and Friedrich Engels published the *Communist Manifesto*, on behalf of a group of idealistic workers. Originally drafted as a programme for an international "Communist League" which had its roots in the 19th-century tradition of workers' mutual improvement societies, it became one of the most important political documents of all time. It has been as influential as the American *Declaration of Independence* (1776) and the French *Declaration of Rights* (1789).

The Communist Manifesto

The **Manifesto** has left an indelible mark on human progress and still today forms the basis for a system of political beliefs that motivates millions. Even after the fall of the Berlin Wall in 1989, and the collapse of Communism in Russia and Eastern Europe, its authority and prestige remain for many. What did it say that seemed so important and revolutionary? The key demands, in the authors' own words, were …

1. Abolition of property in land and application of all rents of land to public purposes.

2. A heavy progressive or graduated income tax.

3. Abolition of all rights of inheritance.

4. Confiscation of the property of all emigrants and rebels.

5. Centralization of credit in the banks of the state, by means of a national bank with state capital and an exclusive monopoly.

6. Centralization of the means of communication and transport in the hands of the state.

7. Extension of factories and instruments of production owned by the state; the bringing into cultivation of waste lands, and the improvement of the soil generally in accordance with a common plan.

8. Equal obligation of all to work. Establishment of industrial armies, especially for agriculture.

9. Combination of agriculture with manufacturing industries; gradual abolition of all the distinction between town and country by a more equable distribution of the populace over the country.

10. Free education for all children in public schools. Abolition of children's factory labour in its present form. Combination of education with industrial production, etc.

THESE DEMANDS WE FOLLOW WITH A STATEMENT OF BOTH PRINCIPLE AND INTENT …

4

> *"If the proletariat during its contest with the bourgeoisie is compelled, by the force of circumstances, to organize itself as a class; if, by means of a revolution, it makes itself the ruling class, and, as such, sweeps away by force the old conditions of production, then it will, along with these conditions, have swept away the conditions for the existence of class antagonisms and of classes generally, and will thereby have abolished its own supremacy as a class. In place of the old bourgeois society, with its classes and class antagonisms, we shall have an association in which the free development of each is the condition for the free development of all."*

It is from these words that, during the next century and a half, revolutionary action swept first across Europe and then across the world.

ALL PROPERTY RELATIONS ARE SUBJECT TO **HISTORICAL CHANGE.** HENCE, SLAVERY HAS RECEDED TO THE PAST ...

CONSIDER HOW MANY OF OUR DEMANDS HAVE BEEN MET, WHOLLY OR IN PART, SINCE 1848.

Brief Life of Marx

Karl Marx was born in 1818 in Triers in the Rhineland of Germany. He was Jewish and came from a line of rabbis but his own father was a lawyer. When he was six, his family converted to Christianity and he grew up a Lutheran.

As a student, philosophy influenced him greatly, particularly the works of **G.W.F. Hegel** (1770–1831). He came to reject the mystical and idealistic nature of Hegel's work and turned to the materialistic ideas of a "Young Hegelian" disciple, **Ludwig Feuerbach** (1804–72). He was soon to move far beyond Feuerbach to the view that the everyday material conditions under which people live actually create the way they see and understand the world.

Meeting Engels

In 1842 he was employed by the *Neue Rheinische Zeitung* newspaper in Cologne and became editor. Within a year, the newspaper had been shut down by the Prussian authorities because of one of Marx's articles. He moved to Paris, then the centre of socialism, and met the influential French socialist **Pierre-Joseph Proudhon** (1809–65) and the Russian anarchist **Mikhail Bakunin** (1814–76) (later to become his greatest enemy). He also met **Friedrich Engels** (1820–95) again.

When Engels introduced himself again in Paris, Marx welcomed him as an intellectual equal and political brother-in-arms.

Together they went on to establish Marxism as an intellectual force. Engels' family were rich owners of cotton-spinning factories in Manchester and Westphalia. He was able to support Marx financially in the hard times to come. But this was not his most important contribution. Marx might have spent his life in an ivory tower of intellectual speculation.

ENGELS BROUGHT ME DOWN TO EARTH. HE KNEW HOW CAPITALISM ACTUALLY WORKED AND THE EFFECTS IT HAD ON WORKING PEOPLE.

IN 1845, I PUBLISHED THE **CONDITION OF THE WORKING CLASS IN ENGLAND.**

Engels also alerted Marx to the importance of Great Britain for the development of capitalism.

The Exile, Agitator and Writer

The Prussian state asked the French authorities to give Marx a hard time. He was duly thrown out of Paris in 1845. He went to Brussels and began a life of political agitation and propaganda.

I WAS ACTIVELY INVOLVED IN THE REVOLUTIONS OF 1848 IN FRANCE AND GERMANY ...

HE WAS EXPELLED FROM GERMANY IN 1849 AND NEVER RETURNED.

Marx even renounced his Prussian citizenship. This may have been a mistake because, some 20 years later, the first serious workers' movement was established there, and Marx was able only to influence it from the sidelines.

Marx lived in London in relative poverty, but always rescued by Engels, for the rest of his life.

Marx died in 1883 and was buried in Highgate cemetery in London. Engels died in 1895 and left everything that he had to Marx's children.

Understanding Marx's Theories

The *Communist Manifesto* was a powerful and coherent call to arms but was not scientific. It provided no thorough theoretical basis for revolution and the end of Capitalism. This would be provided by Marx and Engels' vast output of other books, pamphlets and polemics, some published after Marx's death.

Perhaps the best account of all their thinking is Engels' *Anti-Dühring*. Professor Eugen Dühring was a German Social Democrat with whom they profoundly disagreed.

Published reluctantly as a supplement by the Social Democratic newspaper *Vorwärts* in 1878, the *Anti-Dühring* eventually did more than any other publication to spread the Marxist position amongst thinkers and workers across the world.

The term "Marxism" has had many different meanings in the years since 1848.

These points will be developed in detail as we move through the text.

▶ A *philosophical* basis which derives much from Hegel but which neatly inverts the key central idea of the Hegelian perspective.

▶ A systematic and complex set of economic and political theories which follow from the philosophical position. The most important of these being the *Theory of Surplus Value* and the *Labour Theory of Value*.

▶ A theory of *revolution*.

Three Roots of Marxian Theory

Marx's theories can be seen as extensions and developments of three European intellectual traditions.

V.I. Lenin (1870–1924) himself explicitly recognized this, which is interesting in the light of later attempts to minimize the importance of Western thought for Communism.

Hegel's View of History

Any understanding of Marxism requires an examination of its roots in the Hegelian tradition. Hegel had a unique and radical view of history. Most historians and philosophers prior to Hegel had seen it as a random and contingent series of events linked in a crudely causal way. Hegel, on the other hand, saw history as a process of development. To understand one part demands an understanding of the whole.

OUR UNDERSTANDING OF ONE EVENT CAN BE IMPROVED TO THE EXTENT THAT WE UNDERSTAND ALL THE EVENTS THAT PRECEDED IT.

I ACCEPT THAT. BUT WHAT EXACTLY IS "DEVELOPING"?

The Reality of Ideas

Like Plato (427–347 BC), Hegel thought that the only things that are really real "are ideas".

Hegel claimed that reality was essentially reason and logic – "whatever is rational is real, and whatever is real is rational". There really **is** a cosmic principle of rationality. This implies that whatever actually happens is part of the cosmic plan and therefore ultimately justifiable. Hegel's idea was of great comfort to the Prussian state, who adopted him as official philosopher.

Hegel also believed that questions about the material world are pointless or meaningless. They are only questions about the *ideas* that we have of the material world. Mind is part of nature and the natural is made up of pure idea.

THE ABSOLUTE, THE **ULTIMATE IDEA,** CONTAINS EVERYTHING — INCLUDING OUR OWN EXPERIENCES — AND TIME ITSELF. IT THEREFORE CONTAINS HISTORY.

SO HISTORY IS THE PROCESS OF THE ABSOLUTE "UNFOLDING ITSELF". THE END OF THIS UNFOLDING PROCESS IS THE REALIZATION OF THE ULTIMATELY AND FINALLY REAL ...

WHICH MEANS, IN HEGEL'S OWN TIME, THE PRUSSIAN STATE!

Hegel thought that the most highly developed aspect of the Absolute was the idea of the state. He is blamed for originating the two most potent and dangerous ideas of the 20th century: Fascism, through his veneration of the state, and Communism, through his idea of the inevitability of progress.

The Philosopher's Role

Although Hegel believed in a dynamic and developing system of ideas, with an ultimate and inevitable goal, he nevertheless did not concern himself with the future. He saw no role for himself nor for any philosophers in predicting or recommending a particular future.

WE CAN ONLY HAVE WISDOM IN HINDSIGHT. "THE OWL OF MINERVA (WISDOM) SPREADS ITS WINGS ONLY WITH THE FALLING OF THE LIGHT."

I DISAGREE VEHEMENTLY WITH THAT! THE JOB OF PHILOSOPHERS IS NOT TO REFLECT ON THE WORLD "AS IT IS", BUT TO **CHANGE** IT.

The Dialectic

Hegel's idealism did provide an answer to the question of how precisely the "unfolding of ideas" takes place. The key concept, and the idea most effectively adopted by Marx, was that of the dialectic. We tend to regard a particular idea, or "explanation", or "theory" as something that stands alone. It represents some aspect of reality and is self-sufficient.

IF WE UNDERSTAND HOW A STEAM-ENGINE WORKS, THEN THAT'S ALL THERE IS TO IT. WE DON'T NEED TO KNOW ANYTHING ELSE TO MAKE IT WORK.

THIS IS WRONG. IF WE EXAMINE ANY IDEA CAREFULLY WE FIND THAT IT IS ALWAYS LINKED TO SOME OTHER IDEAS ...

... EITHER BECAUSE IT ACTUALLY CONTRADICTS THEM OR BECAUSE IT SOLVES PROBLEMS OR CONTRADICTIONS IN THE OTHER IDEAS.

CLEARLY, IDEAS OR EXPLANATIONS CHANGE OVER TIME, THROUGH HISTORY.

Therefore, since our world is an idea or set of ideas, the history of our world is actually the history of these ideas and the way they are linked together.

The Dialectic in Practice

Take, for example, the question of why things fall down. Aristotle believed they did so because all things had an innate tendency to go either upwards or downwards. Consequently, the speed at which something falls is determined by two factors, the resistance of the material it is travelling through (generally air or water) and its weight.

ALBERT EINSTEIN (1879–1955)

No doubt, in time, problems with Einstein's theory will arise. Indeed, there are already difficulties in physics to reconcile Einstein's relativity with the science of the really small, of quantum mechanics. Einstein's insistence that light was always at a constant speed is itself now being questioned. The process by which ideas or explanations challenge each other and, in doing so, bring forth another better theory, Hegel called the "dialectic".

The Dialectic in Progress

The term "dialectic" has its origins in ancient Greece. It was seen as a special process of dialogue whereby opposing views or opinions could be reconciled with each other to establish the truth.

Thesis, Antithesis, Synthesis

Hegel thought that every explanation or theory, short of the Absolute, had something wrong with it. Some parts would be either false or incomplete. Therefore another idea would arise which contradicted it, or in his terminology, "negated" it. These two would be in opposition until a third explanation arose which reconciled the two and embraced the good parts of both, abandoning the incomplete or false.

Hegel saw three "Laws" by which the dialectic operated. Marx and Engels were happy to accept all of them. Let's now see what these Laws are.

The First Law

The Law of the Transformation of Quantity into Quality. Things tend to change gradually – *quantitatively* – for the most part, but will sometimes make a sudden leap into a different state. This is a *qualitative* change that can only happen after a period of quantitative change.

The Second Law

The Law of the Unity of Opposites. Many, and perhaps all things in the world exist in opposition. Day and night, hot and cold, good and bad, near and far. But they do not really exist separately to each other. They form unions outside of which neither can exist. Day has no meaning without night, good without bad. The identity of each depends on the identity of the other.

The Third Law

The Law of the Negation of the Negation. Any thesis contains within itself problems and difficulties (contradictions) which will bring about its downfall. This downfall is actually achieved by the antithesis which reveals the contradictions. Thus it negates the thesis. But the antithesis itself contains its own contradictions which are exposed by the synthesis. Thus the negation is itself negated. Marxists identify this process operating in history.

THE FEUDAL SYSTEM CONTAINED STRUCTURAL ELEMENTS THAT INEVITABLY LED TO ITS DOWNFALL.

ITS CONTRADICTIONS WERE EXPOSED BY CAPITALISM. THEREFORE CAPITALISM "NEGATED" FEUDALISM.

In each negation, the contradictions are abandoned but the good things retained. Socialism will abandon the exploitation of capitalism but will retain the advanced technology. In this way the process of the negation of the negation is progressive and optimistic.

The Marxian Dialectic

For Marx and Engels, the dialectic provided a superior kind of reasoning to traditional formal logic. Unlike the latter, it was dynamic, could deal with transformation and could explain how things come into being from nothing. Formal logic was static and seemed to imply that the underlying nature of reality was unchanging. Consequently, previous philosophers had great difficulty in explaining *change*. As revolutionaries, they also saw in the dialectic a requirement to study social phenomena in terms of their context and relationships with each other, to study them in *motion* and *change*, and not as static objects.

Marx regarded the rest of Hegel's work as nonsense. His basic criticism was that Hegel went wrong to say that reality was essentially *mental* – made up of ideas.

THE REAL WORLD IS MADE UP OF **UNTHINKING** OBJECTS THAT ARE SEPARATE FROM HUMANS AND CAN EXIST WITHOUT THEM.

I FOUND HEGEL "UPSIDE DOWN" AND SET HIM THE RIGHT WAY UP.

MANY HAVE SAID THAT MARX OVERSIMPLIFIED AND MISUNDERSTOOD ME.

In the Introduction to the first volume of *Capital* (1867) Marx says …

"My own dialectic method is not only different from the Hegelian, but is its direct opposite. For Hegel … the thinking process is the demiurge (creator) of the real world, and the real world is only the outward manifestation of 'the idea'. With me, on the other hand, the ideal is nothing else than the material world reflected by the human mind and translated into terms of thought."

A Materialist World

So, what we think and how we see the world is determined entirely by the nature of the physical and social reality in which we live. Our ideas do not make the world, the world makes our ideas. Marx is therefore a materialist; Hegel, an idealist.

We might now say that Marx failed, but his work was a towering intellectual achievement.

Marx and Engels believed it was the dialectic that made their theories "scientific", meaning free of mysticism and metaphysics, but also describing something like a scientific "law" which implied a kind of inevitability.

Modernist Optimism

Marx and Engels were also part of a larger movement of the 19th century, "modernism". This was the view that underneath the haphazard and contingent ordinariness of everyday life were certain dynamic powers that, while remaining hidden, controlled the way things changed and determined the future. Essentially materialistic and positivistic (believing in progress through an accumulation of knowledge), modernists determined the character of contemporary Western culture.

My Theory of Evolution is an example ...

My Theory of the Unconscious is another.

SIGMUND FREUD (1856–1939)

CHARLES DARWIN (1809–82)

Even modern physics can be seen in this light.

EINSTEIN

The 19th century gained optimism in the discovery of laws applicable to the improvement of the human condition.

Dialectical Materialism

Materialism alone was not enough for Marx. Enlightenment empiricism had led to a materialistic view of the world as a machine operating according to invariable laws.

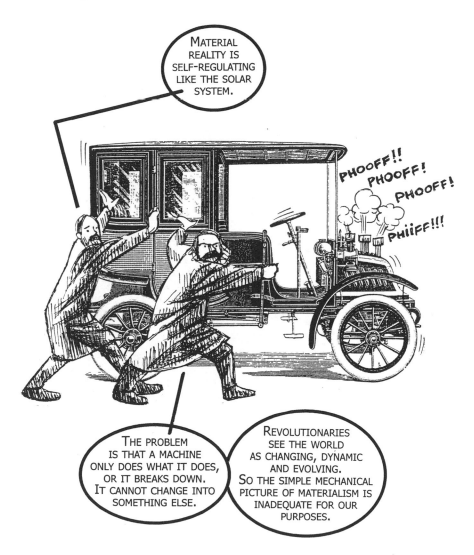

The solution lay in **dialectical materialism**. Using this, the contradictions inherent in all aspects of the world at any one time made the transformation into something else inevitable. Their job was to chart that *revolutionary* inevitability.

The Three Stages

Dialectical Materialism provided all that Marx needed as a basis for a revolutionary theory. It was scientific, it insisted on change, and it could be used to chart a direction from which revolutionary activists could learn. Along with this went a conception of change in human nature, or "species-nature" as Marx called it, that involved **three stages**, or "moments". To begin with, humans are entirely consumed by their "species-life".

THEY ARE JUST ABOUT AWARE OF THEMSELVES. THEY COOPERATE, THEY LIVE FREELY, BECAUSE THEY ARE TRUE TO THEMSELVES ...

BUT DETERMINISTICALLY, BECAUSE THEY DO NOT REFLECT ON, AND ACT TO CHANGE, THEIR CIRCUMSTANCES.

At this point, humans are free in the fullest *socialist* sense because they are able to control their own destiny. They are no longer determined by their natural environment and the antagonisms instigated by necessity.

The Productive Forces

The basic human relations are dictated by the necessity to *produce* and exchange goods that can satisfy the wide range of our needs.

NATURE PROVIDES HUMANS ONLY WITH RAW MATERIALS THAT HAVE TO BE WORKED.

Human labour, their acquired practical skills and implements or machines made to help them extract and transform the raw materials – these Marx calls the "productive forces". But these are not enough.

The Productive Relations

Humans must also work together to be effective. There must be relationships between them. These Marx calls the "productive relations". In early human history, Marx believed, people worked together in a cooperative "primitive communism".

Class Antagonisms

So, the productive relations themselves instil hostility between two fundamental *antagonistic classes* – the exploiters and the exploited. Marx begins the *Communist Manifesto* with that idea:

"The history of all hitherto existing societies is the history of the class struggle."

39

Substructure and Superstructure

The foundations of any society consist of the basic productive forces and relations. Marx called this the *substructure* or *infrastructure* fundamental to materialistic social reality. There is always a *superstructure* of laws, customs, religions, government and other *cultural* institutions whose independence is entirely an illusion. Culture's sole *ideological* function is to protect the interests of the class that owns the forces of production.

FOR EXAMPLE, TODAY, THE INSTITUTIONS OF MARRIAGE AND FAMILY LIFE SEEM THE WAY THAT PEOPLE CHOOSE TO LIVE ...

BUT, IN FACT, "FAMILY LIFE" IS DESIGNED TO REPRODUCE A STEADY SUPPLY OF NEW WORKERS AT NO COST TO THE EMPLOYERS.

Transitions from one kind of society to another happen when some kind of major technological change in the forces of production simply does not fit with the existing *relations* of production. Rapid changes in the way that goods are produced introduce sudden, violent and qualitative changes to the ways that humans relate to each other.

A Question of Economics

To understand these vital social transitions – and in particular the one Marx expected to take place in the transition from capitalism to true socialism – it is necessary to understand the basic elements of his economic theory. This theory is what makes Marxism both compelling and scientific. It explains why so many people for so long took its truth as an article of faith.

Classical British Economics

Marxian science has its roots in classical economic theory developed at the end of the 18th century. **David Ricardo** (1772–1823), the great British economist, had developed a *labour theory of value*.

I REALIZED THAT THE PRICE OF A PARTICULAR COMMODITY DEPENDS ON THE TIME IT TAKES TO MAKE IT.

A PENCIL COSTS 10P AND A PEN COSTS £1 BECAUSE THE PEN TAKES TEN TIMES AS MUCH TIME TO MAKE.

RICARDO SAW THIS SIMPLY AS A GOOD WAY OF EXPLAINING THE **PRICES** OF THINGS IN SHOPS.

Marx, however, saw it as the real key to exploitation and inequality. The essence is in the twin ideas of **commodity** and **value**.

What is a Commodity?

Marx defines a commodity in *Capital* as "a thing that by its properties satisfies human wants of some sort or another". A commodity can be used by the producer or by someone else.

Any commodity can be exchanged for any other commodity, but in very different quantities. A pile of sand is a commodity because it can be used for something, such as building, but it would take a very large pile of sand to be exchanged for even a very small piece of platinum.

The question then becomes, what determines the *ratios* at which all these commodities are exchanged? What is common to them all that determines the rates at which they are exchanged? What is this third thing that they both relate to?

HERE, MARX BEGAN TO BUILD ON RICARDO'S LABOUR THEORY OF VALUE.

THE COMMON FACTOR IS THE **AMOUNT OF LABOUR** WHICH HAS GONE INTO THEIR PRODUCTION.

Or, as Marx states in *Capital*, *"The value of one commodity is to the value of another, as the labour time necessary for the production of one is to the other."*

The Means of Production

The next key factor in the equation is the "means of production", the tools, equipment and machinery used to make the commodity. These change and develop. A new piece of machinery may allow workers to make twice as much of the commodity as they did before. The exchange value of the commodity would then fall by half.

Those who bought the new machinery and made workers redundant were the owners of the means of production, the capitalists, the class of the "bourgeoisie".

The Problem of Profit

However, the capitalists had problems of their own. If they paid their workers the real exchange value of their labour – that is, the *price* of the commodity – then the capitalist entrepreneurs would make no profit, no money and no income.

If a competitor made the same product using new machinery and sold it at half the price, then the original producer would go out of business. No one wants to buy an identical product at twice the cost. People choose to buy things on the basis of quality and price. If the quality is the same for two identical items, they will buy the cheapest.

Profit is not just something that allows capitalists to live well. It is an essential aspect of the whole system. Without profit, capitalism could not survive. Marx needed to explain where the profit came from. To understand his answer, we need to understand two separate economic activities: one carried out by the worker, the other by the capitalist.

The Production System

Workers sell their labour for money, in the form of wages, which they use to buy the things they need, like food, shelter and so on.

As we have seen, a commodity always comes from a process of production that involves two things – the *means of production* (machines, factories etc.) and *labour*. Since commodities are always bought at their exchange value, no more and no less, then the profit must come from the act of production itself.

The money that capitalists must pay for the means of production is largely beyond their control. They have to pay for the machines at their exchange value – what someone will sell them for. The same is true of the raw materials they use in production, the coal, the steel, the plastic. Someone wants a price for them and will not sell for less. Marx called this "fixed capital".

Marx called this "variable capital" because he realized that it was the one element of capital not fixed.

Variable Capital and Labour Exploitation

Profit must come from variable capital. The inevitable exploitation of capitalism takes place. The worker is obliged to work for longer than the real exchange rate of their labour.

WE ARE PAID FOR WORKING SIX HOURS, BUT MADE TO WORK FOR TEN HOURS.

THIS ENABLES ME TO SELL A COMMODITY (A CAR, A PEN, WHATEVER) WITH AN EXCHANGE VALUE THAT CONTAINS WITHIN IT MORE LABOUR VALUE THAN WAS ACTUALLY PAID FOR BY WAGES.

THIS IS MY "THEORY OF SURPLUS VALUE" ...

Fixed capital, machines and raw materials, does not add value to the finished commodity. Such capital is in the exchange value of the commodity but does not increase value. Variable capital, money spent on labour power, does increase the commodity's exchange value because, during the process of production, the workers spend some time working for nothing. The worker puts more value into the commodity than they are paid for. They are exploited.

Absolute Surplus Value

We need to make a distinction between *absolute* and *relative* surplus value. Given a particular kind of technology, the absolute surplus value will simply be determined by the number of hours that the capitalist can get the worker to put in for no wages.

In the 19th century, capitalists made workers put in extraordinarily long hours by our standards. Men, women and children were obliged to keep hours that we would find barbaric, and in appalling conditions. But there is a real limit to what a worker can be made to do before they collapse. They need some rest.

Relative Surplus Value

To make as much profit as possible, capitalists had to find some means of increasing the *rate* at which the surplus value is produced. The only way to do this is to make the workers themselves more productive, without working more hours than they can survive. Possible increases or decreases in the rate of surplus value gave Marx the concept of "relative" surplus value.

This must be done, otherwise another capitalist manufacturer will do the same thing and undercut his competitor.

This increase in the rate of surplus value will almost certainly result in an increase in the quantity of surplus value (profit) because fewer workers will be needed. They can be made redundant, their wages saved, the factory produces more goods in less time and sells them more competitively. More people buy them. The workers lose out.

The Contradiction of Capitalism

In this process of constant effort to increase efficiency and the volume of profit, Marx saw the essential contradiction of capitalism. The process involved a fundamental change in the way that capital was composed. This change would lead to an eventual decrease in the rate of surplus value.

Fixed capital can only put its own value into the exchange value of a commodity. Therefore, in the long run, the rate of surplus value will fall, profits will fall, and capitalists must force workers to work longer for lower wages.

Society must increasingly become polarized between a shrinking capitalist class and a massive proletariat that suffers worsening misery. A crisis point will arrive when this cannot continue and revolution must occur.

The Prophecy

In the first volume of *Capital*, Marx offers his famous prophecy.

"Along with the constantly diminishing number of the magnates of capital, who usurp and monopolize all advantages of this process of transformation, grows the mass of misery, oppression, slavery, degradation, exploitation; but with this too grows the revolt of the working class, a class always increasing in numbers, and disciplined, united, organized by the very mechanism of the process of capitalist production itself. The monopoly of capital becomes a fetter upon the mode of production, which has sprung up and flourished along with, and under it. Centralization of the means of production and socialization of labour at last reach a point where they become incompatible with their capitalist integument. This integument is burst asunder. The knell of capitalist private property sounds. The expropriators are expropriated."

The revolution would be preceded by a series of intensifying crises. Goods would be produced which the impoverished proletariat could not afford to buy. More workers would be forced out of work, because their labour was not needed. This would drive wages down further, lessening still the ability of the people to buy the products of capitalism. Enterprises would collapse and be swallowed by larger organizations in the centralization of capital. At other times, shortages of labour would drive wages so high that the basic profitability of enterprises was compromised.

Organizing Capitalism's Downfall

The process of production itself would help in establishing the basis for revolution. Concentration of capital also meant a concentration of workers. They would come to see their shared position of exploitation and alienation. Marx used the term "class consciousness" to describe this.

TWO FACTORS ARE NECESSARY FOR CLASS CONSCIOUSNESS TO EMERGE ...

FIRST, THERE NEEDS TO BE AN **OBJECTIVE REALITY** OF LARGE NUMBERS OF WORKERS SHARING THE SAME POSITION.

SECOND, THERE NEEDS TO BE A **SUBJECTIVE FACTOR,** AN ACTUAL AWARENESS OF THAT SHARED POSITION AND OF THE EXISTENCE OF ANOTHER CLASS WITH OPPOSING EXPLOITATIVE INTERESTS.

Consciousness of Alienation

As class consciousness emerges, workers become aware of their own "alienation". This is a key term for Marx and is central to his concept of human nature. The working-class proletariat have been alienated throughout the capitalist epoch, without being aware of it. By alienation, Marx means a number of different things. His most detailed discussion of them is in the *Economic and Political Manuscripts of 1844*. To be alienated is to have a fractured or improper or distanced or estranged relationship to something. Marx believed that we humans are not in a proper relationship to the key parts of our lives – to other people, things and activities.

AS A RESULT, WE ARE PERMANENTLY UNHAPPY AND DISSATISFIED.

WE HAVE ONLY THE ILLUSION OF HAPPINESS, BECAUSE IT IS AN ESSENTIAL PART OF OUR NATURE TO BE IN A PROPER RELATIONSHIP TO THESE THINGS.

The Nature of Alienation

Alienation takes a number of forms that are all related to our productive activity. It is in the nature of people to be active and interactive with nature and other people in the process of making and changing things. When these relationships become distorted or estranged from us, we are not fulfilling our nature.

We are alienated from each other, because the productive process of capitalism requires a superstructure of ideas which distorts and obscures the naturally cooperative way that we should relate to other people. For example, capitalism pits worker against worker by installing the "idea" that they are in competition for the same work. Finally, we are alienated from ourselves as a species. This is the most fundamental kind of alienation.

The shelters that we build can be magnificent and varied. As Marx says, "man also produces in accordance with the laws of beauty". Production is essentially social and, in its undistorted form, intrinsically satisfying. It is what we want to do because we enjoy it.

Understanding Alienation

Most humans have to live in conditions that make unalienated, proper relations to life itself impossible. Instead of being a joy and a pleasure, work becomes boring drudgery. We only really feel free in the functions we share with animals – sex, drinking, eating, pleasure. Going on holiday seems to be the only time we are really human and alive. All this leads to a kind of self-alienation. This is by no means a new concept.

The Fetish Concept

Immanuel Kant (1724–1804) provided Marx with the concept of "fetish". Kant distinguished real religious thought concerned with the true nature of God, of man and the relationship between them, from unreal or distorted religious thought. The latter is **fetishism** which describes the way that humans project themselves subjectively onto the world of man-made objects.

We are unhappy in our present state of consciousness because it has been reduced to a commodity relationship that values things, not people. Consciousness must rid itself of all fetishistic traces of religion in the recognition that knowledge can only be found in genuine social relationships and action.

The Categorical Imperative

Marx borrowed another Kantian idea of the Categorical Imperative. This is an essential moral principle. One formulation is that a rational human can never use another simply for his or her own selfish purposes. Others must always be treated as *ends* in themselves and never as *means only*.

IF I TREAT YOU AS A MEANS OF GAINING MY OWN ENDS, I THEN ALSO TURN MYSELF INTO A MEANS FOR ACHIEVING MY OWN ENDS.

THIS IS A DIFFICULT POINT BUT CAN BE ILLUSTRATED BY KANT'S ARGUMENT AGAINST SUICIDE.

IT IS NEVER RIGHT TO KILL MYSELF IN ORDER TO RELIEVE MY OWN SUFFERING BECAUSE I AM THEN USING MYSELF AS A MEANS OF ACHIEVING MY OWN ENDS — THE RELIEF OF MY SUFFERING.

Capitalism, clearly, is a system in which people use each other for their own ends. This is true not least for the capitalists themselves but also for the workers, because their relationships with each other are distorted.

To summarize, a human becomes an *object* for himself, is alienated from himself, when he fetishistically invests objects in the world with what are essentially human powers and characteristics, and when he treats himself and others as means to his own ends rather than ends in themselves.

Under capitalism the private ownership of property, of objects, is the principle of social organization. So objects are fully fetishized.

Money Speaks for Us

The economic system has forced us to treat each other as means and we are all alienated from ourselves. In "On the Jewish Question", Marx says:

> "Money is the universal, self-constituted value of all things. Hence it has robbed the whole world, the human world as well as nature, of its proper value. Money is the alienated essence of man's labour and life, and this alien essence dominates him as he worships it."

Although difficult and ambiguous, it is important to understand the Marxian concept of alienation because, while much else of what he said has been disregarded or is now thought to be wrong, alienation remains at the heart of modern Marxist or post-Marxist thinking, as we shall see.

Birth of the Communist Party

So, in theory, as the proletariat become aware of their alienation and exploitation, they begin the process of becoming a *class for themselves*. During this process, a leadership emerges, the Communist Party. The doctrine of the role of the Party had to wait for Lenin in Russia to be set out in detail, but its foundations lie within Marx's own work.

THIS PARTY WILL LEAD THE WORKERS THROUGH THE REVOLUTION IN WHICH THE CAPITALIST SYSTEM IS FINALLY DESTROYED ...

A COMMUNIST SOCIETY WILL ARISE THAT I CALL THE "DICTATORSHIP OF THE PROLETARIAT".

A TERM I BORROWED FROM THE FRENCH COMMUNIST REVOLUTIONARY **LOUIS AUGUSTE BLANQUI** (1805–81).

Remnants of the old system will be removed. Law, administration, education and social welfare will be remade truly to reflect the interests of the people.

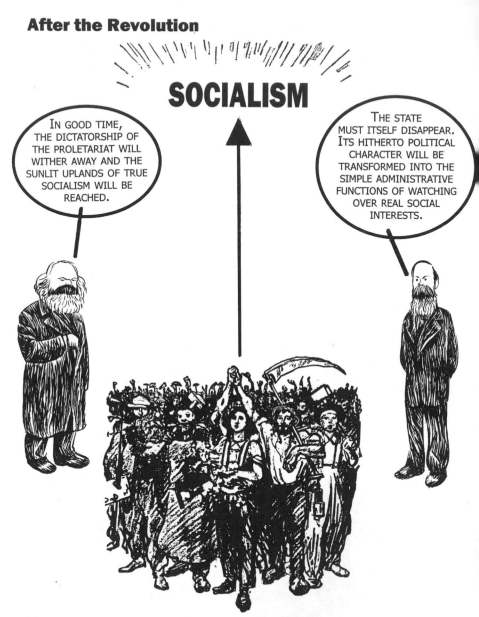

Marx himself is notoriously vague about the details of the post-revolutionary world. Will the dialectic cease to operate and therefore mark the *end of history*? This is very odd. If the dialectic is the inevitable logic of change, then history must also continue to change, presumably beyond Communism. But if the dialectic ceases, then will nothing more ever happen?

What Marx does say is best expressed in his own famous words.

*"In the higher phase of communist society after the enslaving subordination of individuals under division of labour, and therewith the antithesis between mental and physical labour, has vanished; after labour has become not merely a means to live, but has become itself the primary necessity of life; after the productive forces have also increased with the all-round development of the individual, and all the springs of cooperative wealth flow more abundantly – only then can the narrow horizon of bourgeois right be fully left behind, and society inscribes on its banners **From each according to his ability, to each according to his needs**."*

Is Marxism really "Scientific"?

Less helpfully, Marx also said:

> "In communist society, where nobody has one exclusive sphere of activity ... society regulates the general production and thus makes it possible for me to do one thing today and another tomorrow, to hunt in the morning, fish in the afternoon, rear cattle in the evening, criticize after dinner, just as I have in mind, without ever becoming hunter, herdsman or critic."

THAT'S ALL HE HAD TO SAY ABOUT THE PRACTICAL DETAILS OF COMMUNIST LIFE.

WOULD WE BE HAPPY BEING CARED FOR IN THIS HAPHAZARD WAY?

Marxist theory seemed rigorous, logical and optimistic. It held out hope in a century when ordinary workers lived in the most hopeless conditions. But more or less all economists today believe Marx's theory seriously flawed, or, to put it bluntly, wrong.

Marx was not scientific. Neither did he anticipate the way that capitalism would develop. The philosopher **Karl Popper** (1902–94) points out in his book *The Poverty of Historicism* that Marx's key concepts are not capable of being shown to be wrong. Popper considers "falsifiability" to be the hallmark of real science.

IF SOMETHING IS SCIENTIFIC, IT MUST BE LOGICALLY POSSIBLE TO FIND EVIDENCE THAT CAN FALSIFY, REFUTE OR SHOW IT TO BE WRONG.

WE CAN NEVER SHOW THAT SOMETHING IS CERTAIN OR TRUE, BUT WE CAN SHOW THAT SOMETHING IS WRONG.

This does not mean that scientific ideas and theories will be shown to be wrong – many have stood the test of experimentation – but only that it must be *theoretically* possible. Marx's theories fail this criterion. Take the concept of "value". If we assume, as Marx himself did, that there will always be a greater supply of workers than demand for them, then increasing misery can be explained without reference at all to value. We don't know if it is significant and have no way of finding out. Popper thought that the dialectic was mystical, unverifiable nonsense. What was real was simply cause and effect.

The Evolution of Capitalism

Marx also assumed that 19th-century *laissez-faire* capitalism, with individuals and families owning whole enterprises, would continue. He did not anticipate that the middle classes, who he thought would be crushed out of existence by the two monolithic classes of capital and labour, would in fact grow from strength to strength.

Others became managers, paid by the shareholders to manage their investment. The latter group, far from joining the proletariat as Marx expected, felt superior to the class from whence they had been drawn.

The concentration of capital does lead to the "collectivization" of workers. But, against Marx's prediction, it allowed workers to form their own associations – the trades unions. Trade unionism is not dedicated to overthrowing the system but to improving wages and conditions. The political philosophy of "welfare state" Social Democracy grew powerful in the 20th century.

A CENTRAL TENET OF THIS PHILOSOPHY IS STATE INTERVENTION IN THE ECONOMY, EVEN TO THE DISADVANTAGE OF THE CAPITALISTS, IN ORDER TO IMPROVE THE CONDITIONS OF ORDINARY PEOPLE.

SO MUCH FOR MARX'S IDEA OF THE GOVERNMENT ONLY EVER SERVING THE INTERESTS OF THE RICH.

Alienation remains Marx's one idea that applies to a world of growing prosperity and affluence in which people still cannot explain why they are unhappy. We are doing something "wrong" that violates our own nature.

The Long Road to Revolution

The Communist Manifesto of 1848 was written for the Communist League. They wanted revolution now, whereas Marx knew that no revolution of any kind was pending at that time, and he told them so.

> WE TELL THE WORKERS: YOU HAVE TO GO THROUGH FIFTEEN, TWENTY, FIFTY YEARS OF CIVIL WARS AND INTERNATIONAL STRUGGLES NOT ONLY TO CHANGE THE INTERNATIONAL SITUATION, BUT TO CHANGE YOURSELVES, AND MAKE YOURSELVES FIT FOR POLITICAL POWER.

Marx was a convinced internationalist. He saw the nation state as a bourgeois creation. No revolution could take place effectively within the confines of one bourgeois system. Revolution had to be international or it could be nothing. After his break with the Communist League, he had little direct contact with proletarian movements for some years, other than a few lectures on political economy.

The First International

In 1862, there occurred perhaps the most important tea party in history. A group of French workers came to London to see the International Exhibition and met a group of British workers. At the Freemasons' Hall, they had what *The Times* described as "a very excellent and substantial tea". Further meetings of workers from various countries led to the "International Federation of Working Men".

The importance of the First International was that it existed at all. Revolutionary visions abounded at the time, impossible to unite behind one programme, but the International did provide a sense of proletarian unity which had previously been absent. It became very large. 800,000 people were thought to pay dues, and through affiliations to other organizations it could claim a membership of 7 million.

The Paris Commune, 1871

The revolution came sooner than anyone expected, with the Paris Commune of 1871, but its result was to destroy the International. The revolt by Paris workers was put down with great brutality by the authorities.

BUT IT WAS PORTRAYED BY THE EUROPEAN PRESS IN PRECISELY THE OPPOSITE WAY ...

WE, THE REVOLUTIONARIES, WERE SAID TO BE THE BARBARIANS OUT TO DESTROY THE FABRIC OF CIVILIZED SOCIETY.

THE PUBLIC SAW THE INTERNATIONAL AS A MAJOR PLAYER IN THE COMMUNE. THE MIDDLE CLASSES AND MODERATE TRADES UNIONISTS FELT THREATENED. MEMBERS LEFT IN GREAT NUMBERS.

End of the International

Prominent on the barricades had been Blanqui and the anarchist Bakunin. Bakunin was inspirational but disorganized and untheoretical.

The whole episode, including the destruction of the Commune, was a great frustration for Marx. He had done nothing to encourage it, because he felt that it was too soon. Its failure meant, he believed, that the revolution across the world had been set back by years.

Towards the Second International

The pressure for national and international socialist movements continued. In the Reichstag elections in Germany of 1890, the Social Democrats gained about one and a half million votes and 35 deputies. In England, in 1881, **Henry Hyndman** (1842–1921) founded what became known as the Social Democratic Foundation.

I FELL OUT WITH MARX BECAUSE I DIDN'T MENTION HIM BY NAME. MY NEWSPAPER ONLY SPOKE OF "THE WORK OF A GREAT THINKER AND ORIGINAL WRITER".

IN FRANCE, THE PARTI OUVRIER FRANÇAIS WAS FOUNDED IN 1879.

THAT PARTY WAS EXPLICITLY MARXIST BUT COULD NOT ACHIEVE A UNITED FRONT ACROSS THE FRENCH LEFT.

A SINGLE MARXIST PARTY DID NOT EMERGE IN FRANCE UNTIL 1907.

In 1889, there were two congresses in Paris, one for Marxists and the other for non-Marxists. They combined and on 14th July, 100 years after the storming of the Bastille, the Second International came into existence.

Its many non-Marxist recruits did accept Marx's main beliefs, such as common ownership of the means of production, the class struggle and the international nature of that struggle.

We tend to remember Marxism as an inflexible dogma, as it did become under the domination of Russian Communism. But in those days there was flexibility based on the desire to recruit as many workers as possible to the belief in socialism as a real possibility rather than to a belief in a set of rigid doctrinal rules. Any political party or trades union could join as long as they agreed in a very general way with broadly Marxist principles.

The Second International Membership

Only the anarchists were excluded. Marx disapproved entirely of anarchism's approach to socialism.

The Second International was otherwise a mixed bag of socialists with very different opinions and degrees of political organization. Delegates were elected by their own organization and were mandated, instructed, to vote and think in particular ways. The Second International had little powers to control its members. Only in 1900 did it establish a central office.

Weaknesses of the Second International

Another major factor contributed to the relative impotence of the Second International. Western economies were enjoying a consumer boom. In the last quarter of the 19th century, prices of consumer goods fell rapidly as the massive investments of labour, effort and capital earlier in the century began to reap benefits. Wages were also rising.

The Phase of Economism

International trades unions realized that their membership would not welcome the chaos which would follow from the overthrow of capitalism when they were currently doing quite well from it. Marx understood this as "economism", limited improvements in workers' conditions.

Revolution became a theoretical issue and the focus was on achieving practical reformist goals such as votes for all, more democracy, better pay and conditions.

A key player in this drama of socialist political positions was the German Social Democratic Party, the largest and most revolutionary in Europe. Disputes revolved around the conflict between the practical reformers and the theoretical revolutionaries. The outcome of the disputes was to be a signpost for the politics of the 20th century. The 1905 revolution in Russia precipitated a crisis and the party split into three groups.

A reformist group more or less openly rejected Marxist principles and set out to work with capitalist governments.

A moderate centre group was led by **August Bebel** (1840–1931) and **Karl Kautsky** (1854–1938).

Only the third group, led by **Karl Liebknecht** (1826–1900) and the romantic figure of **Rosa Luxemburg** (1871–1919), was explicitly Marxist and revolutionary. It became the German Communist Party in 1918.

Russian Marxism

In Russia, meanwhile, Marxism had become a powerful and well-understood theory. The first part of Marx's *Capital* had been published in Russian in 1872, before anywhere else in Europe.

Looking Ahead

V.I. Lenin, the leading Russian Marxist, recognized that the Second International had achieved something in establishing political consciousness and in helping workers' groups to organize themselves.

From this point, 20th-century left-wingers were divided into Marxists and social reformists. There was never again to be seen the ideological blending and fusion of the 19th century. The Second International was dissolved at a conference in Hamburg in 1923.

Russia's Revolutionary History

Russia's history of revolutionary thought and activity begins in the 19th century. One of the early guiding ideas was that the peasantry must be the revolutionary body, if only because they were so numerous and oppressed.

In 1883 a group of exiles in Switzerland, **George Plekhanov** (1856–1918), **P.B. Axelrod** (1850–1928) and **Vera Zasulich** (1851–1919), established a Marxist group called "The Emancipation of Labour".

Plekhanov's prediction soon proved correct. Capitalism was growing fast in Russia, organized along modern lines with large factories and concentrations of workers.

Lenin went to St Petersburg in 1893 and by 1895 had managed to unite a number of Marxist groups into the "League of the Struggle for the Emancipation of the Working Class".

BUT I WAS THEN ARRESTED AND SENT TO SIBERIA. WHILE I WAS THERE, OTHER GROUPS FOUNDED THE RUSSIAN SOCIAL DEMOCRATIC LABOUR PARTY (RSDLP).

Lenin returned in 1900 and helped to found an illegal newspaper, *Iskra* (The Spark).

Lenin's Bolshevik Faction

Lenin laid out the principles he wanted the RSDLP to adopt in *What is to be done?*, published in 1902. He used these principles to split the Social Democratic Party at their second congress of 1903. His faction became known as the Bolsheviks, while the others were the Mensheviks. The original argument was over membership. Lenin wanted only dedicated and, if possible, trained revolutionaries. The Mensheviks were happy to include sympathizers. The split developed over other issues. Many, including **Leon Trotsky** (1879–1940), changed sides.

The final separation came at a secret conference in Prague in 1912 where Lenin engineered the election of a new Central Committee.

Trotsky's Permanent Revolution

There was also a third smaller faction within the original party. This was led by Trotsky.

UNLIKE THE MENSHEVIKS, I BELIEVED THERE COULD AND SHOULD BE NO COOPERATION WITH THE BOURGEOISIE AND THAT POWER HAD TO BE SEIZED BY THE URBAN PROLETARIAT.

AND UNLIKE LENIN, I HAD NO EXPECTATION OF AN EVENTUAL UNION BETWEEN THE PROLETARIAT AND THE PEASANTS.

I BELIEVE IN "PERMANENT REVOLUTION" – THE IDEA THAT REVOLUTION IN RUSSIA CAN ONLY BE SUSTAINED IF ACCOMPANIED BY REVOLUTIONS IN OTHER DEVELOPED INDUSTRIAL STATES.

This was to make him an enemy of the Stalinist regime in 1930s Russia, and he would be assassinated on Stalin's orders.

Lenin's Revolutionary Marxism

Lenin had to face the reality of revolution that Marx never did. Marx said little about the practical methodology of revolution. He seemed to think that it would take care of itself, somehow. Lenin actually had to carry a revolution through.

In hindsight, Lenin's approach can be seen as excessively doctrinaire. Edmund Wilson described him as "the victim of a theological obsession with doctrine". This misunderstands Lenin's intentions. Lenin had a clear vision of how revolution should be achieved. His "doctrine" was a handbook for how revolutionaries should act, always justified by the appropriate reference to what Marx himself had said.

The Age of Imperialism

Lenin believed that the situation facing Marxists in the early years of the 20th century was significantly different from that on which Marx had based his ideas. Capitalism had entered a new stage, that of imperialism, which Lenin called the "highest stage of capitalism".

THE CAPITALIST SYSTEM DEPENDS ON GROWTH.

IT MUST HAVE NEW MARKETS FOR ITS PRODUCTS TO AVOID THE PROBLEMS OF OVER-PRODUCTION AND DECLINE IN PROFITS.

IT ALWAYS NEEDS MORE AND CHEAPER RAW MATERIALS.

SOUTH AMERICA

AFRICA

"Imperialism is capitalism in that stage of development in which the domination of monopoly and finance capital has taken shape; in which the export of capital has acquired pronounced importance; in which the division of the world by international trusts has begun; and in which the partition of all the territory of the earth by the greatest capitalist countries has been completed."

A New Theory of International Revolution

Lenin foresaw globalization in its primary stages. As the concentration of capital continued and turned into monopolies and cartels, capital would sweep across the world, drawing every country into the system. The monopolies and trusts would divide the world "amicably" between them and, for a time, would prosper.

Experience of Imperialism at War

Imperial Russia had fought and lost a war against Imperial Japan in 1904 and this had precipitated a revolution in 1905. It started in the January, when a peaceful demonstration was fired upon by Tsarist troops.

THE FIRST WORKERS' SOVIET (ELECTED COUNCIL OR COMMITTEE) WAS ESTABLISHED IN ST PETERSBURG IN OCTOBER.

THE REVOLUTION WAS QUICKLY CRUSHED. REFORMS THAT IT HAD FORCED FROM THE TSAR WERE RESCINDED AND I HAD TO FLEE INTO EXILE.

Lenin did not return until 1917 in his famous armoured train. The 1905 revolution really had been spontaneous. It arose from a popular will of the people and was not a creation of the Marxist Bolshevik Party. But the Party learned from it, and all classes of Russian people came to see their own class position. The country became polarized, a precondition for full revolution.

The Two Revolutions of 1917

When the first revolution of 1917 occurred, Lenin had a strategy. Russia was in the midst of another disastrous imperialist war, the First World War. A revolution in the February of that year brought down the Tsar. The following month a Provisional Government was established.

AN ALTERNATIVE OR PARALLEL SOVIET GOVERNMENT WAS ALSO CREATED IN PETROGRAD (ST PETERSBURG) WITH REPRESENTATIVES FROM SOVIETS IN TOWNS AND VILLAGES ACROSS THE COUNTRY.

AT THE TIME, THE BOLSHEVIKS WERE QUITE WEAK.

Lenin returned from exile on 16 April and called for immediate withdrawal of any support for the Provisional Government and the foundation of a Soviet Republic. He famously called for "All power to the Soviets".

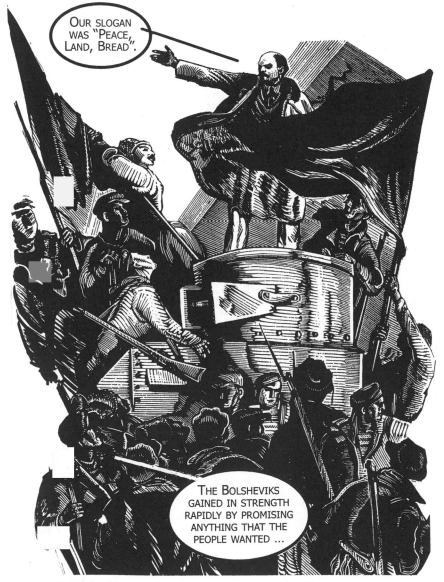

The Bolsheviks also enhanced their reputation by the important role they played in defeating a counter-revolution. The armed forces mutinied and the credibility and power of the Provisional Government vanished. On 25 October 1917 the Bolsheviks easily took power.

The October Revolution

October was not a spontaneous revolution of the people. One relatively small Bolshevik party outwitted another – the Menshevik – because it was better organized, more committed and had a clear view of what to do. The Mensheviks were confused about policy.

The Vanguard Communist Party

A "Dictatorship of the Proletariat" was supposed to be a temporary measure, before the establishment of true socialism and the "withering away" of the state. A left-wing government had as its main task the preparation of the people for the disappearance of government in the normal sense. The state would be administered through the soviets. The Communist Party assumed the role of "vanguard of the proletariat". It would educate the mass of workers and guide them.

The Reality of Communist Control

In fact, the Party's Central Committee was far too large to fulfil its functions and decisions were made by the Politburo (the central policy-making and governing body of the Communist Party). Stalin later exposed the reality.

THE **PARTY** EXERCISES THE DICTATORSHIP OF THE PROLETARIAT …

THE DICTATORSHIP IS IN ESSENCE THE DICTATORSHIP OF ITS VANGUARD, THE **PARTY.**

THE SOVIETS' ROLE WAS SECONDARY TO THE PARTY'S, BECAUSE THERE WAS NO DIFFERENCE BETWEEN THE CONSTITUTION OF THE NEW STATE AND THE RULE OF THE PARTY. THEY WERE "AS ONE".

Trotsky disagreed with this view – another nail in his coffin – because he believed that the revolution had been carried through in the name of the Soviets.

This role of vanguard "party dictatorship" became the model for future revolutions around the world. Other national communist parties were strictly instructed to follow the Russian archetype, often in very different circumstances.

Lenin ceased to function after strokes in 1922 and 1923. He died in 1924. He had, in many eyes, betrayed the revolution, because it had not been truly proletarian. Lenin identified the proletariat with the party vanguard; leadership became subjugation. His successor **Stalin** (1879–1953) completed the process by welding Marxism onto Russia's traditional Asiatic-Byzantine style of autocracy. He became the "Red Tsar".

The Struggle for Leadership

In the issue of Lenin's succession, the leader of the "right" was
N.I. Bukharin (1888–1938) who supported peasant farms, the sale of
some surpluses and the existence of some privately owned workshops
allowed a maximum of only 50 workers. The "commanding heights" of
the socialist economy were to be owned and controlled by the state.

Nevertheless, Stalin won the succession battle. He did this by taking on boring jobs that were actually quite influential. He was General Secretary of the *Orgburo* (Organization Bureau), one step down from the Politburo itself.

This was the so-called "Lenin Enrolment" during which some 300,000 new members were brought into the party as a kind of living memorial to Lenin. Stalin began to remove opponents from their position in 1926.

Stalin's Dictatorship

Stalin became increasingly ruthless and brutal in his search for unlimited power during what he called the "Great Breakthrough" or "Second Revolution" of 1929–33. During the Great Terror (or *Yezhovshchina*) of 1936–9, millions were killed on his orders, including most of those who had led the Bolsheviks with Lenin.

Yet he was seen at first as "Lenin's Apostle" who led the mourning at Lenin's funeral which Trotsky did not attend. Trotsky lost control of the Red Army, which he led in the Civil War that followed the revolution, and was forced into exile.

In the name of "Marxism-Leninism", the Red Tsar enforced the genocidal collectivization of agriculture and the destruction of the Kulak class of relatively prosperous peasants. He pushed for massive industrialization, expecting that war would come with Germany. His deeply suspicious nature turned to paranoia. He introduced a regime based on terror and a huge secret service. Failures were routinely blamed on traitors. History was re-written and the education system subverted. Religion was banned (Marx had called it "The opium of the masses") and a cult of personality replaced it. Roads and towns were named after Stalin and statues, portraits and posters of him were everywhere.

Why Did It "Go Wrong"?

This picture of Soviet life under Stalin is comparable to life in Nazi Germany under Hitler. Both were "totalitarian" in the sense of imposing total demands on their citizens which permitted them no independence: economic, political, social, cultural and psychological. This is not what Marx intended. Stalin froze the progress of the dialectic in a form of "state capitalism" of monolithic inefficiency.

A NEW RULING CLASS AROSE — THE PARTY MEMBER **APPARATCHIKS** AND **NOMENKLATURA** — WHO WOULD FIGHT TO THE END TO AVOID CHANGE ...

WHICH IS WHAT, IN FACT, THEY DID.

WHAT WAS SPECIAL ABOUT STALIN WAS THAT HE WAS A VERY GREAT CRIMINAL.

OR YOU COULD ARGUE THAT THE PARTY WAS AUTHORITARIAN FROM THE START ...

One reason for Party dictatorship can be traced to the Civil War (1918–21), a vicious and costly struggle against "White" counter-revolutionaries supported by Western allies, Britain, France, the USA and others. Lenin began to terrorize anyone who lost confidence in the Communists. He created the CHEKA in 1917, the first Soviet security service, to wipe out all opposition.

Democracy Aborted

Lenin may have begun by working for a democratic socialist society, but he and the Communist Party were corrupted by power during the Civil War. The Party apparatus came to believe that it could trust neither the masses nor even the Party itself. Concentration camps for opponents and political murders were a feature of the regime from the early days.

LENIN ORIGINALLY ENCOURAGED MY ATTEMPTS TO LIBERATE WOMEN AND PROMOTE RADICAL REFORM IN FAMILY LIFE — SUCH AS EASY DIVORCE.

ALEXANDRA KOLLONTAI (1872–1952)
COMMISSAR OF SOCIAL WELFARE

WOMEN WERE SOON DE-LIBERATED IN STALIN'S REGIME AND THE AUTHORITY OF THE FAMILY RE-ASSERTED.

LENIN ORIGINALLY SPOKE OF "THE PEOPLE" CONTROLLING THE BUREAUCRACY.

BUT HIS ATTEMPTS TO CONTROL THE BUREAUCRATS MADE THINGS WORSE BY ADDING ANOTHER LAYER.

Lenin's Legacy

Is there a continuity between Lenin and Stalin or a sudden change between the two? The issue is an important one for Marxist theory and policy in the rest of the world. Many in the West were enthralled by the Russian Revolution and were committed to Marxism. Stalin's excesses turned them against Russian Communism.

The historian Robert Service has said, "Debate rightly exists over the degree and type of continuities that existed between Leninism and Stalinism: and only the wilfully blind would fail to see that those continuities are very strong indeed."

The Conditions of Russia

There is a factor unique to Russia. It always seemed to need an authoritarian leader of immense power who could protect Russia from two threats to which she was particularly vulnerable: foreign invasions and revolts of the peasantry. There are many similarities between Stalin and the former Tsars.

Some have argued that Russia was so backward economically and socially that it needed someone like Stalin to drag it into the 20th century and create a modern industrial state. Isaac Deutscher, in his biography of Stalin, says "Russia had been belated in her historical development. In England serfdom had disappeared by the end of the 14th century. Stalin's parents were still serfs. By the standards of British history, the 14th and 20th centuries have, in a sense, met … in Stalin. The historian cannot be seriously surprised if he finds in him some traits usually associated with tyrants of earlier centuries."

The Kronstadt sailors already attacked Lenin in 1921 for destroying popular democracy and creating a dictatorship long before Stalin came to power. In Aleksander Solzhenitzyn's novel *First Circle* (1968) the hero finds himself in a Stalinist prison camp and complains to older prisoners.

The Soviet Bloc

The nature and constitution of the Russian communist state was set in stone by Lenin and Stalin. Thereafter it seemed incapable of change or development. The expected revolutions in capitalist Western economies never happened. Revolutions instead occurred in the developing Third World, China, Cuba, Vietnam and so on. The only other new Marxist regimes of the 20th century were those created in countries seized by Russia at the conclusion of the Second World War. In these Eastern European nations, Poland, East Germany, Czechoslovakia and elsewhere in the "Eastern Bloc", Communist regimes were installed in the strict Russian pattern.

Socialism in One Country

Perhaps the biggest Russian mistake was the policy of "socialism in one country". Marxism became embalmed in nationalism. Nationalism conflicts with Marx's belief that there can be no other vehicle for the revolution than the *international* proletariat.

TO SUGGEST THAT MEMBERS OF A SOCIETY, WHATEVER THEIR CLASS, SHOULD HAVE AN ALLEGIANCE TO THE NATION STATE, AT A MORE PROFOUND LEVEL THAN THAT OF CLASS, UNDERMINES THE WHOLE MARXIST POSITION.

THE POLICY OF "SOCIALISM IN ONE COUNTRY" IS STALIN'S, AND THE OPPOSITE POSITION OF WORLD REVOLUTION IS MINE.

THE DIFFERENCES ARE THOSE OF DEGREE RATHER THAN FUNDAMENTAL BELIEF.

EAST

Both Stalin and Trotsky wanted world revolution and both wanted well-established socialism in Russia. It's just that for Stalin world revolution came second and Russian socialism first, while Trotsky took the reverse view.

Stalin's Conception of Marxism

Stalin was especially wary of possible counter-revolution. He wanted an absolutely firm and secure national base from which to promote revolution across the world. He claimed that the Soviet State was different to any other and had not been foreseen by Marx, Engels or Lenin. It could not "wither away" until it had reached its highest development. At the June 1930 Party Congress he said, in a characteristic piece of distortion of the original Marxist conception …

"We are for the withering away of the state. And yet we also believe in the proletarian dictatorship, which represents the strongest and mightiest form of state power that has existed up to now. To keep on developing state power in order to prepare the conditions for the withering away of state power – that is the Marxist formula. Is it 'contradictory'? Yes 'contradictory'. But the contradiction is vital and wholly reflects the Marxist dialectic …"

The Cold War

The regimes of Soviet Russia and its Eastern bloc became isolated, rigid and inward-looking. The threat, rather than the reality, of world revolution provoked fear and sustained hostility in the Western democratic "free world". An era of Cold War ensued, from 1950 to 1990, in deadlock between US-led "free enterprise" capitalism and Russian-style state socialism.

Third World Marxism

Many ostensibly Marxist regimes were established in the mid-20th century, often through revolutionary force, across the developing Third World. These tended to follow the orthodox Soviet pattern, often because their leaders had been educated in Russia and because they greatly depended on Russian economic and military support. Revolution also relied on "cult of personality" figures, such as …

Mao Tse-tung (1893–1976) in China
Revolution 1949
▼

WE WERE INFLUENCED BY OUR OWN SPECIFIC LOCAL CIRCUMSTANCES …

OUR REVOLUTIONS WERE INVARIABLY STRONGLY NATIONALIST.

Ho Chi Minh (1890–1969) in Vietnam
Revolution 1954
▶

◀ **Fidel Castro** (b. 1926) in Cuba
Revolution 1959

The peculiar character of revolution in industrially underdeveloped China was perhaps more representative of Third World state socialism than the Russian model.

MY REVOLUTIONARY THEORY DEPENDED FOR ITS SUCCESS ON THE HUGE MASS OF PEASANTS — BECAUSE THERE WERE SO FEW INDUSTRIAL WORKERS.

THIS IS CONTRARY TO MY CLASSICAL THEORY OF RELIANCE ON THE INDUSTRIAL PROLETARIAT ...

SUCH THEORY CEASES TO BE MARXIST AND BECOMES SIMPLY "REVOLUTIONARY", WITH A MARXIST GLOSS.

After Mao's death, and his regime of horrific terror, China has begun to accommodate itself to some capitalist "reform".

The Failure of Marxism

Also by the mid-20th century, it became clear to most observers outside the Communist Bloc that classical Marxist theory had failed.

MY PROPHECY OF "INEVITABLE REVOLUTIONS" IN THE INDUSTRIALIZED COUNTRIES OF THE WEST PROVED INCORRECT.

THE MIDDLE CLASSES HAVE GROWN HUGELY AFFLUENT RATHER THAN BEING SQUEEZED INTO POVERTY.

THE EXISTING COMMUNIST COUNTRIES ARE NIGHTMARES OF INHUMANITY AND INEFFICIENCY.

SOMETHING IS WRONG WITH MARX'S ORIGINAL THEORY.

The most likely flaw was in Marxism's *economic determinism* which elected the industrial proletariat as the only force able to make the revolution because of "iron rules of economics".

Two factors contributed to rethinking Marxism in this chaotic century. One stemmed from theorists working within the Marxist tradition and often within the Communist parties themselves. The other came from a movement of re-evaluation that came to be known as postmodernism. We will look at each of these to see how an alternative "new" Marxism and post-Marxism have emerged.

Gramsci Confronts Fascism

A pivotal figure in the development of classical Marxism is the Italian communist, **Antonio Gramsci** (1891–1937). His work was written largely after he was sentenced to life imprisonment by Mussolini's Fascist dictatorship in Italy in 1926. He elaborated the concept of **hegemony** which attempts to explain not only why workers might not be revolutionary but why they could turn Fascist.

Gramsci wanted to eliminate this economic determinism and replace it with explanations of social change that lay in the superstructure – in the realm of *ideas* rather than economy.

Ideology and Hegemony

A key idea was "ideology". Marx called this a "false consciousness". We can define this as the set of attitudes, values and perceptions through which we come to understand and relate to the given world.

Gramsci emphasized the role of human agency and choice, while maintaining the Marxist reality of class struggle. He claimed that the class struggle must always take place through ideology. Ideas could bring about the revolution – or equally *prevent it*.

The capitalist bourgeoisie class were able to dominate the proletariat in two decisive ways. One was through obvious economic domination, the threat of a lost job, or sheer force. But the other way was to control the ideas, the ideology, of the workers. Gramsci gave the name *hegemony* to this control of ideas which manipulates social consciousness. His insight was that economic and physical force alone was not enough to ensure control.

HEGEMONY CAN BE CHARACTERIZED IN THIS WAY.
▶ Agreement from the majority of a society for the "picture of life" that is represented by those in power.
▶The values, both moral and political, involved in this agreement will be largely those of the ruling class.
▶ The ideology comes to be seen as evident "commonsense" by the majority of people. It becomes "natural" to think like that.
▶ The consent is arrived at largely peacefully, but physical force can be used to support it against a dissident minority, so long as the majority acquiesce.

Hegemony changes over time as it readjusts to changing circumstances. It is the product of a kind of negotiation between the dominant and the controlled class over what the latter will accept to believe and what they will not swallow. The British aristocracy in the 20th century found that the mass of the people would not accept them as hereditary rulers.

Culture, Ideology and Hegemony

It helps to be clear about the relationships between the terms "culture", "ideology" and "hegemony". Culture is usually taken to mean the whole set of attitudes, values and norms that bind a particular society together into a working unit. However, according to Marx (and Gramsci), to see this in a morally neutral way is mistaken.

The question then becomes one of seeing exactly how this transformation from culture and ideology to hegemony can take place. In the past, key institutions for establishing the hegemony have been the Church and cultural institutions, such as the education system.

This insight is one later to be adopted by most Marxist and post-Marxist thinkers, such as the Frankfurt School, the postmodern social theorist **Michel Foucault** (1926–84), Louis Althusser and Stuart Hall.

Control of Hegemony

Hegemony is not only a method of control for the ruling capitalist bourgeoisie. The proletariat can use it to their own advantage. But they cannot do it alone. They need to work with other disadvantaged and exploited groups.

THESE OTHER GROUPS SHOULD NOT HAVE THEIR OWN FREEDOM AND CHARACTER SUBSUMED BY THE ORGANIZED MARXIST MOVEMENT.

THEY AND THE MARXISTS NEED TO MAINTAIN THEIR INDEPENDENCE.

It was in this spirit that the leftwing students and industrial workers combined in France in the famous events of 1968. All groups can make their own special contribution to the struggle and form a popular collective will.

But remember Gramsci's point. Physical force against a minority of dissidents can be used to re-establish consensus, if the majority acquiesce. This is what happened in 1968. The student unrest, in alliance with the workers, nearly brought down President Charles De Gaulle's government.

Gramsci's idea is that revolution can take place only if there is a genuine *alternative world view* accepted by the widest range of exploited groups.

Revolution and Democratic Society

Gramsci thought that a frontal attack on an unpopular autocratic regime, such as Tsarist Russia, had a good chance of success. But in liberal democratic societies the struggle would be longer and would involve ideas and culture, rather than just politics and economics.

The importance of Gramsci for alternative Marxism is that he made everyday culture political, an arena for struggle and not simply a product of economic determinism. But he remains nevertheless a Marxist constrained by its theoretical structure.

The Frankfurt School

Gramsci's name is associated with the emergence of the "New Left" in the 1960s, that is, modern Marxism. Equally important was the early contribution of the Frankfurt School. This is the common name given to the members of the Institute for Social Research, founded in 1923 in Frankfurt, but which emigrated to New York in 1933.

Here are some of the best-known associated directly or indirectly with the Frankfurt School.

T.W. Adorno (1903–69) (philosopher, sociologist and musicologist), **Walter Benjamin** (1892–1940) (essayist and literary critic), **Herbert Marcuse** (1898–1979) (philosopher), **Max Horkheimer** (1895–1973) (philosopher and sociologist) and, later, the philosopher and sociologist **Jürgen Habermas** (b. 1929).

Critical Theory in Dark Times

The Frankfurt circle had witnessed the rise of Stalinist Russia and its perversion of Marx, the rise of Italian fascism, of Nazism and the Holocaust, the A-bomb, the Cold War and the hegemony of America.

WE KNEW THAT THE HORRORS PERPETRATED IN THE NAME OF THE WORKERS AND WITH THEIR APPARENT ACQUIESCENCE COULD NOT BE RECONCILED WITH TRADITIONAL MARXISM.

WE RECOGNIZED THAT SOMETHING MUST BE DONE TO ADJUST MARXISM.

ITS THEORY MUST CHANGE TO FIT THE EXPERIENCES THAT THE WORLD HAS UNDERGONE IN THIS DREADFUL CENTURY.

OUR IDEAS BECAME KNOWN COLLECTIVELY AS "CRITICAL THEORY".

Conventional Marxists called them "revisionist", a term of abuse, because of their attack on the crudely materialistic economic determinism of the old school. Like Gramsci, the Frankfurt School emphasized that the nature of human consciousness was not entirely driven by material conditions.

They have been accused of a bourgeois "élitist" fear of the moral, cultural and physical debasement of society which would follow from the increasing power and influence of the masses. But they made their diagnosis Marxist by identifying cultural "debasement" as the result of manipulation by the capitalist-owned and driven mass media.

Critical Theory of the Media

They foresaw at an early stage in the 1930s the media's power to create ideologies of the world. The media would destroy the workers' ability to make revolution.

"The means of … communication …, the irresistible output of the entertainment and information industry carry with them prescribed attitudes and habits, certain intellectual and emotional reactions which bind the consumers … to the producers and, through the latter to the whole [social system]. The products indoctrinate and manipulate; they promote a false consciousness which is immune against its falsehood … Thus emerges a pattern of one-dimensional thought and behaviour."
H. Marcuse, *One-Dimensional Man*

Social Research for Revolution

Adorno and Horkheimer particularly wanted to produce a new "Critical Theory" method of studying society which would have the potential for producing revolutionary action. This involved the combination of various existing social sciences into one theoretical tool.

THE ESSENTIAL WAS TO CLOSE THE HISTORICAL GAP BETWEEN ACADEMIC "HIGH THEORY" AND BASIC EMPIRICAL SOCIAL RESEARCH.

REALITY

REASON

THE TWO STRANDS OUGHT TO MEET IN SUCH A WAY THAT THE EMPIRICAL ANALYSIS OF REALITY COINCIDES WITH THE PHILOSOPHICO-HISTORICAL CONCEPTION OF REASON.

Collecting facts endlessly is sterile and unproductive, designing bigger and more elaborate theories is self-indulgent. This was a harsh but justified criticism aimed at Marx.

The Hegemonic Role of Culture

Marcuse and Horkheimer hoped that this fusion of disciplines, a tight linking of theory and research, would produce a "critical theory" pointing to necessary revolutionary activity. It would also help to explain some puzzling facts.

WHY DID REVOLUTION FAIL TO HAPPEN IN THE 1930s, WHEN THE GREAT DEPRESSION SWEPT THE WORLD, AND CAPITALISM SEEMED TO FAIL?

WHY WAS REVOLUTION UNLIKELY TO HAPPEN IN THE FORESEEABLE FUTURE?

The "commodification" of all forms of culture – turning all its aspects into saleable things – and the rise of mass communications meant that not only was revolutionary potential capable of being deflected, it could also be turned to reactionary or Fascist ends.

137

Althusser's Anti-Humanism

Louis Althusser (1918–90), the French Marxist philosopher, moved even further away than the Frankfurt School from economic determinism. In the 1960s, he explicitly rejected Marx's essentialism. "Essentialism" is the belief that major aspects of reality can be explained by reference to one underlying essential principle.

I ABANDONED TWO SEPARATE ESSENTIALIST POSITIONS: ONE WAS ECONOMIC DETERMINISM, BUT THE OTHER WAS MARX'S HUMANISM.

Humanism is the view that social change reflects a pre-given and essentially fixed human nature. Rather than imagining a human essence, we ought to think of *structures* in which humans are compliant – hence why Althusser is known as a "structuralist" Marxist.

Instead of human nature, we humans have ideology alone. Ideology structures consciousness and is determined largely by "ideological state apparatuses", such as the church, the legal and education system, the media. These ideological state apparatuses have some degree of freedom of their own and are not just simply tools of capitalism.

Althusser says ideology "represents the imaginary relationship of individuals to their real conditions of existence". The dominant ideology sucks in the individual (Althusser's word is "interpellates") so that the world cannot be seen in any other way.

The Shift to Postmodernism

As with the Frankfurt School, critics have argued that Althusser's picture of the "media apparatus" is too monolithic. People are not simply brainwashed into mindless compliance. They remain capable of projecting meanings onto the media "texts".

There is no restriction on the ways we can interpret. This criticism of Althusser represents the view of "postmodernism" and, along with the New Left, has been influential in forming what is now known as Post-Marxism.

A post-Marxist position from within the left-wing tradition was developed by the British sociologist, Stuart Hall, in the 1960s and 70s at the Birmingham Centre for Contemporary Cultural Studies. Working with Gramsci's theory of Hegemony and Althusser's concept of the ideological state apparatus, Hall does see the mass media as paramount in generating the "pictures of reality" that support the ruling class. But he also sees the media as "a field of ideological struggle".

The ruling class does not have its own way all the time. It too must work within the media to maintain its dominance in the face of opposition from the traditional working class, but also from other groups such as blacks and women.

The Turning-Point in Marxism

Until the New Left revival in the 1960s and 70s, revolution and social change had to come in practice from the mass industrial proletariat. Thereafter, in the socio-economic arena and the ideological battleground, the workers gave up their primary role as the leaders of the revolution and became one group among many. Hence, the classic theory veered to post-Marxism.

Postmodernism's roots can be traced to problems of scepticism and relativism that date back at least to ancient Greece. The question is: "Do we, or can we if we try very hard, see the world as it *really is*, or are the contents of all our experiences entirely mental, made of appearances?" The history of philosophy is in no small way a history of this debate.

All great philosophers have had a go at this one and none have been successful.

"Is Anyone There?"

For the late 20th century, the name for the anti-realist position was postmodernism. Its particular relativist focus is that we can only make sense of the world through *language*. Language is the fundamental means by which we comprehend things. As Wittgenstein put it, "Whereof we cannot speak, thereof we must remain silent."

Without language we, thinking and deciding human people, would not *be there*. Language is what makes us human and different from animals.

We could draw a handy realist conclusion from this, if we were sure that language matches the world, but it doesn't. Words in every language change their meaning all the time. Language is unstable and not attached to any particular reality. As I write, a war in Iraq draws to a close – a particularly fertile time for words to lose and change their meanings as different groups with different interests challenge each other over events, the "reality" of which we will never know.

In a Post-Industrial Era

We might suppose that the idea of "narrative" and the idea of "ideology" are much the same. But traditional Marxists resist any dilution of classic theory with postmodern ideas. The Marxist critic **Fredric Jameson** (b. 1934) argues that modern industrial society is actually *post-industrial* society.

> THE OLD DAYS ARE PAST OF MASS INDUSTRIAL PRODUCTION IN FACTORIES — AND THE SUPERSTRUCTURE OF IDEAS AND CULTURE HAS CHANGED AS WELL.

> POSTMODERNISM ITSELF IS A "CORRESPONDING CULTURAL STYLE" TO POST-INDUSTRIAL SOCIETY.

> JUST AS PRODUCTION HAS FRAGMENTED AND DISPERSED, SO WE ALSO THINK IN MORE FRAGMENTED AND DISPERSED WAYS OF SEEING THE WORLD.

But it is still capitalism, still exploitation, still class-based. Postmodernism is not a "historical rupture" as French sociologist **Jean Baudrillard** (b. 1929) has said, but a product of late capitalism. It is itself an ideology.

The basic division between Marxism today and postmodernism, whether they give primacy of position to ideology or language or narrative, is on the issue of *direction*. Marxists still insist on evolutionary movement and change based on a doctrine of material relations and social action. Postmodernists deny that there is any particular direction, and also deny the existence of "material truth". Marxists today would accept the importance of narrative and discourse but insist that an understanding of these must take place within a context of *materialistic determinism*.

For postmodernists, there is no "subject" of consciousness; no "personal identity" as a private, unified thing on which texts, interpretations and perceptions can impinge.

Seeing the Patterns

Marxists hate this kind of thinking. For them, truth exists and can only exist by virtue of the existence of a conscious subject. A contemporary writer on Marxism, Roger Gottlieb, has said: *"Conceiving of reality and personal identity as endlessly interpretable texts ignores the crucial structural differences between texts and other parts of the world. Texts, for one thing, are not only systems of meaning capable of interpretation. They are also physical artefacts which are produced, exchanged, and owned under particular social relationships."*

So, however readers might interpret a newspaper article about a strike, the important thing for Marxists is that it is in a newspaper which is owned and controlled by someone who has a "hegemonic" point of view and wishes to promote that view. Postmodernists cannot see *patterns* in society.

The End of History

Contemporary events bear them out. Conservative American thinkers from sociologist **Daniel Bell** (b. 1919) after the Second World War to political scientist **Francis Fukuyama** (b. 1952) more recently have confidently predicted the "end of ideology", the "end of conflicts" based on deeply held principles. Fukuyama in particular has had a major impact on current thinking. His world view was detailed in his book, *The End of History and the Last Man* (1992).

There is no need and no possibility in Fukuyama's view of progressing beyond this, and hence no need for ideology. Liberal democracy is the non-ideological, objective reality of the end of human history. He is no naive evolutionist and recognizes that progress towards this goal will be intermittent and difficult, but he sees the broad direction of human progress in these terms.

Clearly this amounts to a rejection of the whole Marxist interpretation of history. Yet, curiously, and as he himself acknowledges, Fukuyama's view of what "History" actually is coincides with the views of both Marx and Hegel.

"And yet what I suggested had come to an end was not the occurrence of events, even large and grave events, but History: that is, history understood as a single, coherent, evolutionary process, when taking into account the experience of all peoples in all times. This understanding of History was most closely associated with the great German philosopher G.W.F. Hegel. It was made part of our daily intellectual atmosphere by Karl Marx ...

Both Hegel and Marx believed that the evolution of human societies was not open-ended, but would end when mankind had achieved a form of society that satisfied its deepest and most fundamental longings. Both thinkers thus posited an 'end of history': for Hegel this was the liberal state, while for Marx it was a communist society. This did not mean that the natural cycle of birth, life, and death would end, that important events would no longer happen, or that newspapers reporting them would cease to be published. It meant, rather, that there would be no further progress in the development of underlying principles and institutions, because all of the really big questions had been settled."

Conflicts are in Progress

Nevertheless, in spite of Fukuyama's optimism about the end of ideological conflict, discord within liberal democratic societies themselves (let alone any others) shows no signs of going away. Opposition to globalization and genetic modification of living things, and the protection of the environment bring thousands out onto the streets in non-violent and violent protest. Revolution is advocated daily by a significant minority, Islamist or otherwise, on a global scale. The internet seems able not only to promote the "dominant ideology" but to provide multiple opportunities for the co-ordination of oppositional activities and subversion. This constitutes a serious criticism of Fukuyama's position.

"IN ZIMBABWE, TRADE UNIONISTS WHO HAD PEACEFULLY GATHERED TO SUPPORT STRIKING DOCTORS AND NURSES WERE ARRESTED."

IF LIBERAL DEMOCRACY REALLY IS THE END POINT OF HUMAN HISTORY, TOWARDS WHICH ALL CHANGE PROGRESSES, THEN WHY IS IT SO DIFFICULT TO ACHIEVE?

WHY DON'T WE ALL JUST BECOME LIBERAL DEMOCRATS NATURALLY?

WHY DO PEOPLE FIGHT SO HARD TO RETAIN ALL THEIR OLD IRRATIONAL RELIGIOUS, NATIONALIST AND MILITARISTIC IDEOLOGIES?

STOP RACISM

STOP THE WAR

NO GM

DO ATTAC IRAQ   NOT IN MY NAME   N IN NA   DON'T ATTACK IRAQ

Deconstructing the End

The strong suspicion remains that "liberal democracy" is itself another ideology, the ideology of late capitalism.

Perhaps the most powerful argument against the "End of History" comes from the French "deconstructionist" philosopher Jacques Derrida. He thinks that Fukuyama's (and Marx's and Hegel's) conception of history is quite wrong.

THEY ALL SEE HISTORY IN A MODERNIST WAY, LOOKING FOR OBJECTIVELY EXISTING "UNDERLYING DYNAMICS" WHICH PUSH HISTORY IN A PARTICULAR DIRECTION.

HISTORY FOR THEM IS "REAL" AND SEPARATE FROM HUMANS. IT EXISTS IN THE WORLD, OVER TIME, AS A SEQUENCE OF IDENTIFIABLE EVENTS.

Against "Truth Claims"

Derrida rejects this interpretation of a "separately existing" history completely. He believes that language, all language, is fundamentally unstable and that "meanings" are, in his own words, "undecidables". The interpretation of language is more like a free-wheeling game-play than a truth-seeking logical analysis. There is no "final" Truth to be found underlying language.

Historians give an account of the past which is rooted in their own subjective experiences and in their own here and now. It is an account of *how they think*, not of how things actually were. Fukuyama's account is an account of his own optimistic ideology.

The Spirit of the Letter

It might follow from this that Derrida advocates a non-political stance to human affairs. After all, if what he says is right, then how can we make any moral or political choices? But in fact Derrida is an "agnostic" postmodernist who remains sympathetic to Marxism. In his book *Specters of Marx* (1994) he defends the *Marxian spirit* rather than the Marxist theory.

PUBLISHED JUST WHEN COMMUNISM HAD FINALLY COLLAPSED ACROSS EUROPE AND MARXISM WAS AT ITS LOWEST POINT ...

YES, AND I MADE THE POINT THAT WHILE CONCEPTIONS OF HISTORY AS EMBODYING REASON AND ENLIGHTENMENT, SUCH AS YOUR OWN AND FUKUYAMA'S, ARE NO LONGER CREDIBLE, HISTORY WILL NOT GO AWAY.

Raising Marx's Ghost

Baudrillard, following roughly the same lines of thought as Derrida, claims that we should content ourselves with living in a permanent "anarchic" present. Derrida knows that this is impossible. We are products of our past, or rather of interpretations of our past. We cannot exorcise the ghosts of the past any more than we can forget our own identities, because *who we are* is made up of these ghosts.

REMEMBER THE WORDS I USED TO OPEN **THE COMMUNIST MANIFESTO**: "A SPECTRE IS HAUNTING EUROPE – THE SPECTRE OF COMMUNISM."

MARX AND MARXISM HAVE BEEN A PART OF OUR CONSCIOUSNESS FOR TOO LONG FOR THEM TO DISAPPEAR IN FUKUYAMA'S "ENDIST" PUFF OF SMOKE.

The analogy that Derrida uses is that of history as "old cloth" that has always to be undone and remade. The past does not contain "decisive ruptures" when an old era ends and a new one begins, because all change is sewn into the tapestry of ordinary lives and ordinary understandings.

It was precisely because of the fall of Communism that it is right that we should revisit Marx – "Not without Marx, no future without Marx, without the memory and the inheritance of Marx: in any case of a certain Marx, of his genius, of at least one of his spirits."

Derrida protests that "… never have violence, inequality, exclusion, famine, and thus economic oppression affected as many human beings in the history of the earth and of humanity." Derrida wants Marxism as a "link of affinity, suffering and hope".

Marxism as an Ethical Programme

Can we go any further in a reconciliation of postmodernism and Marxism? One way of solving the problem for Marxists would be to agree with Derrida and shift from a scientific system to a moral system. Post-Marxists would have to shift from making declarations from within an objective science to a position of making injunctions from within an ethical programme. Instead of saying that such and such *will* happen, they could say such and such *should* happen, so that Marxism becomes an ethical system.

THE PROBLEM WITH THIS POSITION IS THAT MORAL SYSTEMS ARE IN ENOUGH TROUBLE ALREADY.

DAVID HUME (1711–76) EMPIRICIST PHILOSOPHER

A.J. AYER (1910–89) LOGICAL POSITIVIST PHILOSOPHER

FACTS OF THE WORLD

THERE ARE NO MEANS OF CROSSING WHAT I CALLED THE "IS-OUGHT GAP", OF MOVING FROM A STATEMENT OF **FACT** TO A STATEMENT OF **VALUE**.

THE CLAIM THAT THE WORKERS, OR ANYONE ELSE, ARE BEING EXPLOITED BECOMES SIMPLY AN EXPRESSION OF AN EMOTIONAL FEELING THAT A PERSON HAPPENS TO HAVE — "HURRAH FOR THE WORKERS! BOO TO THE CAPITALISTS!"

Most people would not be satisfied with a theory of social change which rested only on emotions, although all would recognize that emotion plays a part.

Defining Post-Marxism

No doubt if "post-Marxism" is accepted it will, like postmodernism, lose the hyphen. The term belongs to the Marxist political philosophers Ernesto Laclau and Chantal Mouffe. In 1985, they published *Hegemony and Socialist Strategy: Towards a Radical Democratic Politics.* This book is difficult and challenging, mainly because what they are attempting to do is create a new way of talking about Marxism.

By Way of Difference

Laclau and Mouffe retain an ethical and moral dimension, as has always been the case in Marxism, and emphasize in particular the idea of justice and fairness. However, they also retain its "objectivity", but they do so in an odd, postmodern way. They want to give an objective account of the mechanisms controlling what is socially and economically "real" …

BUT OBJECTIVITY IS ONLY ONE PART OF THE REAL IN TOTAL HUMAN EXPERIENCE.

WE TRY TO MAP THE WAY THAT "OBJECTIVE KNOWLEDGE" GAINS ITS SPECIAL STATUS.

WHAT HAPPENS TO MY DIALECTICAL MATERIALISM?

They replace the old Marxian dialectic with a methodology derived from modern "deconstructive" linguistics, in which something comes to be defined through what it is not, on the basis of "difference". The Swiss linguist **Ferdinand de Saussure** (1857–1913) proposed that signification arises from *arbitrary differences* – /c/a/t/ and /r/a/t/ signify their meanings by the different single phonemes 'c' and 'r'.

The Dance of Différance

Derrida coined the word **différance** which has no dictionary meaning in French. It is intelligible only as a "play"-word oscillating between *differing* and *deferral*. He is highlighting the reality that linguistic meaning has gaps, absences and postponements: it never resides in one sense only.

Post-Marxist Antagonisms

Laclau and Mouffe want to save Marxism from itself and certainly save the idea of freedom from exploitation and subjection which seems always part of capitalist production. The "post" in post-Marxism is about the abandonment of the essentialist aspects of Marxism and means "other than" or "more than" Marxism.

Antagonisms can arise through class, but are just as likely to do so through gender, ethnicity, sexual orientation, age, locality or anything else. Postmodernism denies the existence of an individual person and sees you or me as a collection of narratives.

Antagonisms are Situated

The result is a view of a society constantly in conflict, with antagonisms running against, across and alongside each other, making strange enemies and stranger bedfellows.

Revolution becomes impossible because a unity of two competing classes cannot be achieved. When attempted, revolutions always end badly.

The State and Civil Society

Classes themselves, in a post-industrial world, are decomposing and degenerating. People no longer feel their class as the primary aspect of their identity – if they ever did. On the other hand, for post-Marxists, the *state* remains the enemy. It is hostile to freedom and democracy, is always corrupt and is unable to deliver social welfare efficiently.

The state will always try to subordinate civil society. Any form of central planning should be avoided.

Solidarity and sympathy within groups and across groups is a humanitarian duty and gesture. A belief in class solidarity is harmful to this process.

Natural "Agonistic Pluralism"

Laclau and Mouffe are truly radical because they want to politicize the whole of life. Power relations are everywhere and have a multiplicity of causes, some economic, some not. They need to be struggled over everywhere. What has been wrong in the past has been to confine politics to the ghetto of the formal democratic process, and thus alienate it from ordinary people.

"Agonistic", from the Greek *agon* meaning "contest", is added to pluralist civil society.

Conflicts between groups, in which each group attempts to impose its own narrative, to its own advantage, should be seen as a natural and normal feature of society. Conflict is restless: alliances will change, causes will change, there will be no stability.

Antagonisms are the product of individual experience and are no more explainable that the experience of the colour yellow.

Where do we end?

In any case, what would a society be like where all conflicts had been resolved and all was perfect harmony? For Laclau and Mouffe, it would be a science-fiction nightmare.

A problem remains of making post-Marxism a programme of civil society based on the ethics of antagonisms. It poses a complaint by Marxist critics also addressed to Derrida's ethical view of post-Marxism: "What is left of Marxism to offer organized resistances to state power and global capitalist economics?"

We began this book with the 10-point programme of the *Communist Manifesto.* We might end by a contrasting 10-point criticism of Marxism in our postmodern world.

1. Socialism does not work and neither does any other grand narrative. The ideologies associated with them are always false.

2. Classes are degenerating and disappearing and attempts to explain things in terms of them are reductionist and wrong. There are many other significant sources of identity and conflict, such as gender, ethnicity, sexual preference.

3. The state as such is always dangerous and cannot deliver effective social welfare; this can only be done by civil society.

4. Any form of central planning is inefficient and tends to corruption; markets are the only mechanism which allows for fair distribution.

5. The old left approach to politics always ends in authoritarian regimes which crush civil society. Politics should exist only at the local level, with local struggles over local issues.

6. Conflicts (antagonisms) are inevitable and while some may be resolved, this merely transforms and clears the ground for further, newer antagonisms. An overview of all conflicts and their eventual resolution is impossible. All we can have are understandings of particular situations at particular moments.

7. This is a good thing, since the resolution of all conflicts would result in a stale, rigid society. An ideal would be a pluralist democracy, providing a stable framework for many local conflicts.

8. Revolutions either cannot happen or end badly. The alternative is democratic transition.

9. Solidarity can exist within and across a range of different groups, it is a humanitarian gesture. A belief in class solidarity as the only valid form of solidarity is harmful to this process.

10. In an interdependent, globalized world, anti-imperialism has had its day. The world is too complex.

To be continued ...

Key Words in This Text

The Absolute: Hegel believed that the progress of the dialectic would end in the establishment of the one final and perfect idea, called "The Absolute".

Agonistic Pluralism: A post-Marxist view that societies today should foster democratic and low-intensity conflicts between a variety of different groups.

Alienation: A Marxist term suggesting that, in a class-based society, humans are fundamentally separated from their activities, themselves and human nature.

Autocracy: A form of government in which total power lies in the hands of one person. The term can also refer to a state ruled in this way.

Bolshevism: A political belief held by the Bolsheviks in Russia which later became the basis for Soviet Communism. The Bolsheviks were more extreme than their milder rivals, the Mensheviks.

Bourgeoisie: Marx's term for the owners of capital. They were able to use this capital, in the form of factories, machinery etc., to make profit.

Capitalism: An economic system of production in which a minority class who owned the means of production were able to exploit the majority to make profit.

Class Consciousness: A class's awareness of their own identity and of their potential.

Commodity: Anything that can be bought and sold. A commodity always has "exchange value" which is put into it by human labour.

Communism: In its widest sense, Communism is a society without money, without a state, without property and without social classes. However, the term has become associated with the particular kind of Marxism found in 20th-century Russia.

Critical Theory: A term with many different applications. Best seen here as a broad movement in the Marxist tradition which takes into account many of the criticisms that have been made of Marxism.

Dialectic: Originally a Greek method of reaching the truth by argument. Adopted by Hegel to describe the way in which ideas evolve through competition with each other.

Economic Determinism: The view that human history is driven by economic factors, rather than by contingent events or by ideas.

Enlightenment: A period usually taken to be around the 18th century in which many contemporary progressive ideas in science and modern philosophy had their origins.

False Consciousness: A set of beliefs held by a class of people that deceived them about their true position.

Falsificationism: A scientific doctrine which holds that a theory or explanation can only be held to be scientific if it has the potential to be shown to be wrong.

Fetishism: In Marxism, the tendency that people have to invest ordinary objects with a special or even spiritual quality. It refers particularly to commodities.

Feudalism: Socio-economic system in which land was owned by the aristocracy and most people were tied to the land, and so worked for the aristocracy. (pp. 38–9)

Hegemony: The way that a ruling class can control a subordinate class by persuading them that the ruling class's own ideological view of the world is "commonsense" and natural. (pp. 121–7)

Idealism: The view that the content of all experience is mental. It follows that the only "reality" lies in ideas. (p. 30)

Ideology: A set of attitudes and values which determine the way in which a class or group of people relate to the world. (p. 120)

Imperialism: For Lenin, the final stage of capitalism, in which the whole world is divided up into competing capitalist camps. (pp. 93–5)

Interpellation: Althusser's term for the way in which people recognize themselves in certain groups, identify with them and are drawn into them. (p. 139)

Laissez-Faire: Unplanned, uncontrolled and unrestricted capitalism. It means "let be" or "let alone". (p. 74)

Materialism: The view that fundamental reality is made up of the inanimate material objects of the world. Mind is dependent on the nature of the material world. (pp. 30–31)

Means of production: The factories, machinery and so on by which commodities are produced. (pp. 46–7)

Modernism: An attitude rather than a theory which suggests that complex aspects of reality such as history, evolution and the human mind can be understood by reference to relatively simple underlying factors and rules. (p. 32)

Nomenklatura: The "ruling class" in the former communist Russia. (p. 106)

Post-Marxism: A recent set of ideas which moves away from Marx's economic determinism and primacy of class but which retains the need for natural human solidarity. (p. 159)

Postmodernism: A sceptical attitude to the modernist position in which the possibility of "true" theoretical explanations of how the world works is denied. (pp. 142–8)

Proletariat: In a capitalist society, those that do not own the means of production and are therefore forced to sell their labour in order to survive. (p. 50)

Relations of Production: Social relationships established to suit a particular mode of production, such as feudalism or capitalism. (p. 37)

Social Democracy: The view that capitalism is inevitable and that the duty of government is to regulate it and protect the weakest. (p. 75)

Substructure: In Marxism, the underlying economic forces that determine the way a society is and the direction of its change. (p. 40)

Superstructure: The social and legal structure which exists above the substructure and about which people retain the fiction that it is in control. (pp. 40–41)

Surplus Value: The value of a product for which the worker is not paid, hence the profit. (pp. 52–5)

Text: For postmodernists, the "text" is anything that can be interpreted – a book, a film, a speech, etc – and reflects a theory of linguistic analysis. (p. 140)

Further Reading

There are very many books about Marx and Marxism. The danger is of drowning either in secondary sources or in material too focused on one issue. Publications on development in the Third World often have some Marxist dimension. I have tried to remain with central texts.

"Lenin and Philosophy" and Other Essays, Louis Althusser, Monthly Review Press (2002). Gives an interesting perspective on Althusser's views on Marx.

A Marx for Our Times: Adventures and Misadventures of a Critique, Daniel Bensaid, Verso Books (2002). A difficult but valuable academic book defending Marx from a postmodernist position.

Althusser and the Renewal of Marxist Social Theory, Robert Paul Resch, University of California Press (1993). An account of Althusser's crucial role in the development of a modern Marxism.

Dictionary of Marxist Thought, Tom Bottomore, Blackwell Publishers (1991). Very useful on terminology.

Early Writings, Karl Marx, Lucio Colletti (Introduction), Rodney Livingstone (Translator), Gregor Benton (Translator), Penguin Classics (1992).

"What Is to Be Done?" and Other Writings, Vladimir Ilyich Lenin, Dover Publications (1987). Lenin's essential grand plan for the revolution. A bible for revolutionaries for decades.

From Hegel to Marx: Studies in the Intellectual Development of Karl Marx, Sidney Hook, Columbia University Press (1994). An old book (first published 1932), but very good on Marx and Hegel.

From Marx to Gramsci, Paul Le Blanc (Editor), Humanity Books (1996). A useful collection of readings.

Hegemony and Socialist Strategy: Towards a Radical Democratic Politics, Ernesto Laclau and Chantal Mouffe, Verso Books (2001). The key book in understanding post-Marxism. Very difficult.

Karl Marx, Francis Wheen, Fourth Estate (2000). An excellent biography.

Karl Marx: Selected Writings, Karl Marx, David McLellan (Editor), Oxford University Press (2000). A good start.

Karl Marx's Theory of History, G.A. Cohen, Oxford University Press (2001). A classic contemporary defence of Marx's economic determinism.

Lenin, Robert Service, Pan (2002). Good political and personal biography.

Main Currents in Sociological Thought, Volume 1, Raymond Aron, Transaction Publishers (1998). A classic. The section on Marx is very helpful.

Marxism After Marx: An Introduction, David McLellan, Palgrave Macmillan (1998). Another classic account. Very reliable.

Marxism and History: A Critical Introduction, S.H. Rigby, Manchester University Press (1998). An interesting account which sees Marxism as raising questions rather than providing answers.

Marxism and Media Studies: Key Concepts and Contemporary Trends, Mike Wayne, Pluto Press (2003). A defence and reinterpretation of Marxism for the modern media world.

Postmodernism: Or, the Cultural Logic of Late Capitalism, Fredric Jameson, Verso Books (1992). An attack on postmodernism and defence of Marxism.

Reaction and Revolutions: Russia 1881–1924 (Access to History), Michael Lynch, Hodder Arnold H&S (2002). Good, straightforward history.

Specters of Marx: The State of the Debt, the Work of Mourning and the New International, Jacques Derrida, Routledge (1994). A radical postmodern reinterpretation of Marxism.

Stalin: The Court of the Red Tsar, Simon Sebag Montefiore, Weidenfeld & Nicholson (2003). The "inside story" of the reign of Stalin.

The Communist Manifesto, Karl Marx et al., Oxford Paperbacks (1998).

The Condition of the Working Class in England: From Personal Observation and Authentic Sources, Friedrich Engels, Penguin Classics (1987). Engels' own account of how it was for workers in the 19th century.

The German Ideology, Karl Marx and Freidrich Engels, Laurence and Wishart (1970). Contains a concise account of a number of their key ideas.

The Revolution Betrayed: What Is the Soviet Union and Where Is It Going?, Leon Trotsky, Pathfinder (1937). Trotsky was Stalin's rival, both in politics and personally. Stalin had him killed.

The Theory and Practice of Communism: An Introduction, R.N. Carew Hunt, Penguin Books (1983). A really useful book, but difficult to get hold of these days.

Understanding Foucault, Geoff Danaher et al., Sage Publications Ltd (2000). A useful interpretation of this major French thinker.

Victor Serge: the Course Is Set on Hope, Susan Weissman, Verso Books (2001). An interesting biography of a man at the centre of communism in the 20th century.

About the Author

The author has been teaching Marxism to a range of students from A level to undergraduates since 1976. He is currently a lecturer in philosophy at a College in south-west England.

He would like to thank Richard Appignanesi and Ruth Nelson for their editorial skills and his wife Betty and children Abigail and Joshua for their encouragement and support.

About the Artist

Oscar Zarate has illustrated many books in the *Introducing* series including Freud, Psychoanalysis, Freud Wars, Existentialism and Kierkegaard. He is currently working on a graphic novel for *Editions Dupuis* in Paris.

Index